Tim and Mits

By Debbie Croft

I am Tim.

I am at my pit.

It is Mits!

I pat Mits at the pit.

Mits! Sit at the pit!

Mits sat.

Mits sat at the tap!

CHECKING FOR MEANING

1. What did Tim do at the sandpit? *(Literal)*

2. Why did Tim call out to Mits? *(Literal)*

3. Why do you think Mits sat at the tap? *(Inferential)*

EXTENDING VOCABULARY

I	Look at the word *I*. Why is the letter *I* always a capital letter when it is by itself? What other words do you know that always start with a capital letter?
pit	Look at the word *pit*. What sounds are in this word? What is the last sound in the word? What other words do you know that end with the same sound?
tap	Look at the word *tap*. What other words do you know that have the *–ap* ending?

MOVING BEYOND THE TEXT

1. When have you played in a sandpit? What did you do?

2. What other pets do people have?

3. If you could have any animal as a pet, what would you choose? Why?

4. What activities make you thirsty like Mits at the end of the story?

SPEED SOUNDS

Mm	Ss	Aa	Pp	Ii	Tt

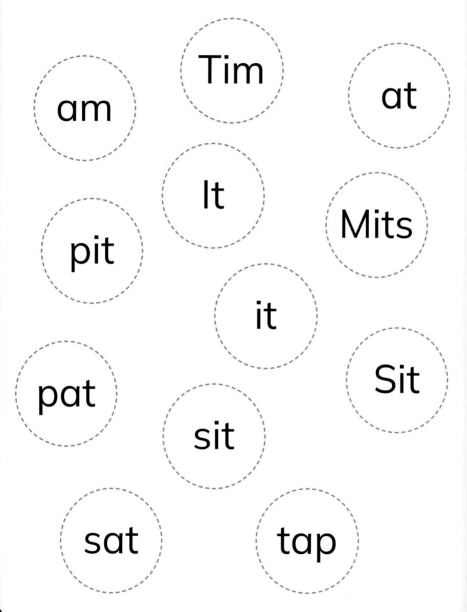

am

Tim

at

It

pit

Mits

it

pat

Sit

sit

sat

tap